I0416105

Atheism with Regards to Government

Anarchy as an Ultimate Given

Why What We Use as Money Matters Volume IV

David Mint

Copyright © 2012 The Wilcox Trading Company

All rights reserved.

ISBN: 1491202343
ISBN-13: 978-1491202340

Cover design by David Mint at WDesign

Adaptation of a stylized anarchy symbol

This volume is dedicated to the peacemakers, wherever they may be.

CONTENTS

ACKNOWLEDGMENTS

First and foremost, we wish thank to the Living God for giving us life and allowing us to encounter the answers to many of life's burning questions. We would also like to thank our wife, children, parents, and extended family who have supported us during this project in innumerable ways, from providing challenging questions to simply listening to us as we processed the many and varied themes explored in these volumes.

We are also indebted to the many writers, teachers, philosophers, and champions of the ideas that this volume borrows from and builds upon.

Finally, we are indebted to all individuals who, despite overwhelming odds, have kept the flame of real freedom burning throughout history, no matter what the cost. It is our hope that these volumes may honor their sacrifices by lighting the torch of freedom for many generations to come and inspiring those same generations to go and do likewise.

DAVID MINT

INTRODUCTION: ANARCHY AS AN ULTIMATE GIVEN

An·ar·chy -/ˈanərkē/- noun -1.a: absence of government b: a state of lawlessness or political disorder due to the absence of governmental authority c: a utopian society of individuals who enjoy complete freedom without government 2.a: absence or denial of any authority or established order b: absence of order 3. atheism with regards to government

Anarchy. The word strikes fear in the hearts general public, who have been trained to conjure images that range from fraternity house shenanigans to rioting and looting on the streets of important cities at its mere mention. For most civilized persons, with these mental images close at hand, anarchy is something to be avoided at all costs. After all, how can civilized society carry on with the threat of bombs and looting effectively slamming the brakes on human progress?

In this volume, we seek to free the concept of anarchy from these negative connotations. For anarchy, far from being the greater evil in the choice amongst evils when it comes to man's state in this world, is really not a choice at

1

all. Rather, anarchy is something that every human being and animal on the planet is born into. It is the basic state of man in this world. It is an ultimate given.

As an ultimate given, it is futile for men and women to live their lives fretting about the society in which they live falling from a state of order into one of anarchy. This line of thinking is debilitating and counterproductive to what must be seen as mankind's highest and most urgent calling in the physical realm: How best to respond to the state of anarchy in which they live.

For it is not anarchy itself that causes disorder and the various maladies which the mere mention of the word bring to mind, but mankind's failed responses to this ultimate given under which they labor and cause others to labor on their behalf. The only thing more dangerous than confusing anarchy for the disorder which arises from the collapse of a failed response to it is to spend one's life toiling under another person's failed response to his or her inherently anarchic surroundings.

Further, this volume seeks to give the reader a sufficient level of awareness to step back, if even for a moment, and evaluate the response to anarchy under which they are currently laboring and make a sober evaluation as to whether they are truly laboring in alignment with their own best interests.

Too many lives have been wasted laboring under a mistaken fear and avoidance of anarchy, and we hope this volume will steer the reader away from this fate. It may not change the way you think or what you do at all, and that is good. For to personally validate ones own course in life with a firmer grasp of the facts has caused harm to no one. In fact, it should cause one to carry on with a renewed sense of pride and purpose. If you find yourself in the camp of self-validation, we encourage you to offer others the chance to give their own lives a sober evaluation, and respect as well as encourage their decision to change once they truly understand the wonderful anarchy into which we are all born.

~~~~~~~~~~~

PROLOGUE: PORTLAND'S BAN ON BISACKSUALS

There are certain questions which one encounters in everyday life that demand a shocking answer.

For example, the everyday grocery bagging inquiry *"Would you like paper or plastic?"* can be responded to with one's customary preference of grocery transport. This is the routine response and requires no creativity whatsoever.

A prepared, slightly creative individual may think outside of the box and have their response prepared. *"I don't need a bag, I've brought my own,"* which in today's environmentally conscious age may be interpreted to mean *"I am saving the earth and thereby reject your greedy corporate attempt to deliberately pollute it by rudely offering me an already manufactured bag for my own convenience."*

Then there is the creative genius, the one who rises above the imaginary philosophical bickering and takes what is given to them while at the same time disarming the mythical compulsion which the slightly creative person above felt threatened by. What is their shocking response to this common question?

"I'll take either one, I'm bisacksual."

In the same way, when approached with the somewhat common question posed by an eager petitioner *"are you registered to vote?"* One can give the standard yes or no answer that the question requires.

The slightly creative person may turn the question into an opportunity to share their point of view. *"That depends, what is the issue?"* Depending upon the issue, they may either wholeheartedly lend their support and sign the petition or engage in a lengthy debate about the error in supporting the proposed legislation.

Enter the creative genius, as in the grocery checkout line, they rise above the imaginary philosophical bickering about what the government should or shouldn't require everyone to do and at the same time disarm the mythical compulsion that caused the slightly creative person to enter into a lengthy and meaningless debate. What, then, is their shocking response to this question?

"I'm an atheist with regards to government."

This volume is dedicated to the creative geniuses.

We currently reside in Portland, Oregon, where plastic bags are frowned upon to the point that the City of Portland passed an ordinance intended to reduce the use of them[1]. The result is that large retailers in Portland are now one-sack outlets, which not only clashes with Portland's tendency towards plurality in any number of

---

[1] More on this ban can be read at:
http://www.oregonlive.com/portland/index.ssf/2011/07/portland_ad opts_ban_on_plastic.html

spheres, but also has noticeably diminished the overall quality of the paper sacks that are now one's only option at many retailers.

The great irony in the ban on bisacksuality is that the same people seen at City Hall protesting the "*forced*" use of plastic bags are likely to be the same ones who will chain themselves to a tree when the increased demand for paper sacks resulting from this action (the butterfly effect, if you will) leads to the acceleration of the destruction of rainforests in the Amazon.

On the bright side, the plastic bag ban and resulting plea to save the rainforests should combine to help Oregon's ailing lumber industry in the short term.

Yet all of this nonsense about plastic bags, the rejection of bisacksual Portlanders, and the backdoor stimulation of the Oregon lumber industry serves to illustrate the effects that government actions have on both the general population and industry.

The government can hardly be blamed, though. For a government, at its base, is nothing more than the incarnation of the collective response to the anarchy in which we live.

~~~~~~~~~~~

DISSENT IS INFORMATION: THE PRIMARY REASON FOR THE SUPERIORITY OF ANARCHY AS A SYSTEM

Anarchy is the primary state of being for all humans, whether we recognize it or not. The sooner one realizes that they live in a state of Anarchy, the better able they will be to operate within it.

More often than not, mankind collectively seeks to confront and manage these inherently anarchic conditions by employing varying degrees of centralized control mechanisms known as government.

However, centralized control, when exercised without consent, is bad for all involved, both for would be controllers as well as for those being controlled.

Fortunately, anarchic systems have a way of dealing with centralized control by forcing the disbandment of any form of control that is not obtained by assent. Not by assent of the majority, as democratic thought would have us believe, but by the assent of each affected individual. As such, if one is involuntarily subject to a form of centralized control, there is an easy escape for those who are not physically detained. The escape hatch is conveniently located in the mind of each individual, as all centralized control mechanisms can be escaped by changing one's mind about the power the mechanism holds over them.

As both Anarchy and its antithesis, centralized control, coexist to some extent all around us in various forms of ultimately voluntary capitalist and socialist systems which are constantly interacting with each other, it is often difficult, if not impossible, to understand why a state of anarchy can be superior to centralized control.

Charles Hugh-Smith recently wrote an essay on Zerohedge.com entitled, *Why Centralization Leads to Collapse*[2], which articulates what we believe to be the primary reason the for the superiority of Anarchy as a system (or non-system, as it were):

Dissent is information

Hugh-Smith, in a concise, well-written piece, recognizes that centralized control, which is a natural outgrowth of the desire for efficiency, leads to the rejection and ultimate termination of viewpoints that do not agree with the ideology or methods of the central authority. Under central control, dissent is ignored, hindered, and in extreme cases, terminated.

However, in suppressing dissent, the centralized authority

---

[2] You can read Mr. Hugh-Smith's entire article here at Zerohedge.com: *Why Centralization Leads to Collapse* at the following link: http://www.zerohedge.com/node/475826

has removed perhaps the most important means by which a system can transmit vital information from the margins to those who may need to act upon such information.

This marginal information is important, as are the activities that dissenters carry out, for their diverse and seemingly contrary activities serve to make the entire system in which people live "*antifragile*," (to borrow the title of the recent book by Nassim Nicholas Taleb, author of the recent bestseller *The Black Swan*). This means, for practical purposes, that an anarchic system is better prepared to deal with changes in data and the natural environment because it is constantly dealing with it by default, while a centralized system labors under the delusion that's contingency plans are adequate to stave off any event that would threaten the supposedly superior system.

The rejection of dissent, then, ensures the collapse of the centralized system, while the tolerance inherent in an anarchic system ensures its resilience. It may be said that the chief virtue of Anarchy, then, is its prevention of centralized control.

~~~~~~~~~~~

THE FOLLY OF FAITH IN GOVERNMENT

As Henry Hazlitt astutely observed in his classic *Economics in one lesson*, actions taken by central governments have the exact opposite long term effect on reality as that which was intended. For this reason alone, all government mandates must be met with suspicion, regardless of the nobility of their intentions.

Yet none of these government actions and the resulting imbalances would be possible without an unwavering faith in the government on the part of the people, which is why the only hope for the world to escape the crazy cycles inherent in placing faith in the government is for the populace to become not militant, but agnostic towards the actions of their government, as they would a well intentioned but clumsy sidekick.

For government, as we have stated before, is simply the incarnation of a collective response to anarchy. The incarnation will resurrect itself for as long as the collective seeks a uniform response to the problems presented by living in an inherently anarchic environment. The only way to truly overcome what we classify as failed responses to anarchy, which is what all governments eventually become, is to embrace Anarchy as an ultimate given and learn to operate in it as an individual. Then, and only then, can groups of experienced individuals hope to mount a coherent response to their anarchic surroundings as a collective.

Take the example of Portland's plastic bag ban. Were the disenfranchised bisacksual population of Portland to violently oppose the plastic bag police (which, most certainly, do not exist), they would be wasting their time and resources only to perpetuate a system which promises nothing more but endless power struggles and the short lived thrill of victory or agony of defeat.

Even if bisacksuality were to be again made legal, no sooner would the ink be dry on the new ordinance than would a band of sacktivist warriors covered in plastic armor be organizing to take back their right to a paper only Portland. The bisacksuals would then organize and revolt, and so on.

To be clear, we personally have no strong feelings one way or the other on the sack issue, we have merely chosen to shamelessly embellish upon the theme in order to make a larger point.

The point is that militancy breeds militancy, and violence breeds violence. Constant power struggles are symptoms of the disease of a forced collective response to anarchy.

Champions of non-resistance, such as William Lloyd Garrison in 19th century America, and more recently Ghandi and Martin Luther King, Jr., understood that long term, permanent change could never come about by force of arms. Rather, they understood that the only way to test whether or not an idea was an imperative of natural law or simply a rule born of temporary public opinion was to live in peaceful defiance of the idea and tolerate whatever opposition they met with. If the collective were indeed right, they would eventually encounter natural barriers to impede their actions. If the collective were wrong, it would ultimately employ force to stop them.

In the case of King, the good reverend was thrust into the civil rights battle in the Southern US. For those who may be unfamiliar with this piece of history, we will oversimplify it by saying that there were rules in the South that demanded that African Americans be segregated from White Americans in various aspects of public and private life. Amongst these was a rule that required African American riders to sit towards the back of the public buses.

Rosa Parks and thousands of other African Americans began to put this rule to the test, not by petitioning the powers that be for permission to sit in front of the bus, but rather, by sitting in front of the bus as if the rule did not exist.

Would some supernatural force come and move her to the back of the bus? Or would those who used the rule to gain privilege for themselves be the ones who would force her to the back of the bus or even deny her entry onto the bus in the first place?

The creative geniuses amongst us already know the answer.

The deeper question that must be addressed, then, is not whether or not each individual rule is necessary, but rather, is a government that imposes rules and forces those affected to comply with those rules a necessity? Or is it merely an imaginary framework used to erect a series of rules that are imposed by one group on other groups in order to gain or maintain an unearned privilege?

The only valid way to test this theory would be for one to live their life as if the government did not really exist. What if one were to test this theory not by withdrawing from the government or fighting to change it, for both courses of action would be to acknowledge its existence, but by simply deciding not to believe in the government? What if one decided to stop attributing power to the government by simply changing their own mind about its existence and acting accordingly?

In other words, what if the simplest path to freedom were to become an atheist with regards to government?

~~~~~~~~~~~

THE KINGDOM OF GOD IS WITHIN YOU

"I am an atheist with regards to the world's governments, for I have chosen to live in the Kingdom of God"

A ride through Portland's plastic bag ban, bisacksuality, the virtues of non-violent protest, Anarchy, atheism, and the imaginary construct of government has lead us to an uncomfortable confrontation with our inner anarchist. Isn't Anarchy a bad thing? Aren't anarchists generally bad people, who wish destruction and chaos in place of the order that we now enjoy?

In the previous chapter, we have proposed that the best way to test the legitimacy of government, that is, its right to govern, would be to simply live as if the government did not exist and see where resistance came from.

If resistance were to come from a majority of individuals who are directly affected by one's actions, then that would lend credence to the necessity and legitimacy of government. If, however, resistance were to appear in the form of a minority relying on an imaginary framework to create and enforce a series of rules that are imposed by one group on other groups in order to gain or maintain an unearned privilege, the legitimacy of the government must be called into question.

For if the government does not work to assist people in working together to form adequate responses to their naturally anarchic state, it is hindering them. There is no neutrality when it comes to claiming a sovereign right over individuals. The claim of this sovereign right implies, by default, that the sovereign entity, in our example the government, will have an impact on the actions of the individual. If this is not the case, the sovereign right is nothing more than an illusion.

Not that it is necessarily the legitimacy of those who are governing at the time that would be questioned, although it is implied, but rather the legitimacy of the apparatus which allows such rule by the minority at the expense of the majority. If a majority would be materially better off by simply shedding the illusion of government, why does the idea of government persist as a seemingly permanent part of the collective conscience?

To briefly answer this question, for it demands a response, the idea of government and its companion, central banking, have risen as mans' collective response to help him deal with his anarchic surroundings. As the idea of government seems to address what would be man's chief preoccupations, were he to acknowledge that he stands naked before the anarchic forces around him, it is natural that this idea would be ingrained in the man's psyche to such an extent that it would drive not only a majority of his own decisions, but also those of his descendants.

Let's face it, it is nice to sleep at night with the idea that someone is watching over our assets and our livelihood. Even more comfort may be had in the idea that, were something to happen to our assets or our livelihood, we would still be taken care of.

Yet given the inherent uncertainty, what we now know as Anarchy, in which we all are obliged to operate, most thinking humans would only dare ascribe the ability to provide universal care to an omniscient and omnipotent deity. Why, then, would it make sense to attribute the power of an all-powerful and all seeing deity to what generally amounts to an assembly of fallible men?

Ever since Adam and Eve were kicked out of the Garden of Eden, men and women have confronted a world that is in a state of anarchy. Given that anarchy demands a response, men and women tend to quickly submit to whatever promises them protection from these anarchic forces. Once they have made the choice to submit, it is extremely difficult to change paths. These yokes to which persons willing submit are commonly known as religion and patriotism. However, if one recognizes that there is an opportunity to change paths, as those who have arrived at this point in this volume most likely have by now, the implications are staggering.

Is it indeed possible to be an atheist with regards to the world's governments? Is it possible to not toil for or against them, but simply to view life as an exercise in dealing with the inconveniences which appear as a result of a large part of the world's population acting upon the belief that the government really exists?

To paraphrase Paul in the Biblical book of Romans, is it possible to live in the world but not be of the world by merely transforming one's way of thinking? For this is the essence of living in the Kingdom of God. As Tolstoy chose to title his magnum opus, so we submit to those who are able to accept it: *The Kingdom of God is within you.*

The only way to know whether or not this staggering choice truly exists is to peacefully and actively test the hypothesis of a government's legitimacy. How can these tests be performed?

~~~~~~~~~~~

THE TEST

In the previous chapter, we presented a hypothesis for dealing with the world's governments. Namely, living as if the government does not exist and seeing where the resistance, if any, comes from. Now, we must move the hypothesis down a level. How, then would one test the hypothesis by embracing Anarchy, or atheism with regards to government, in a place like Oregon?

Oregon is a State that places a relatively large amount of faith in its political system and, by extension, the power of the government to solve social problems.

The approach seems to work for most. The territory is home to an abundance of natural resources and a great number of people who are willing to go along with the government's program. In these conditions, the idea and mechanisms of government are tolerated and to an extent championed, for it is possible to live in Oregon and enjoy a relatively high standard of living despite the waste inherent in governmental activities.

However, one can only wonder as to what might be here in the great Northwest were the government not to hyper regulate every industry or confiscate 9% of the wages earned by its laborers on top of the roughly 21% that the Federal government lays claim to.

Is the average citizen better off living on just 70% of their wages? Or, put another way, does the average citizen derive enough benefit from being governed that he or she would value it at roughly one third of his or her income?

There are burning questions that every citizen would do well to ask of themselves, if not their government, from time to time. If the mechanism of government were to go away, or be reduced to the spheres where it paradoxically does add value to the economy (note that, were this the case, it would technically cease to be government, per se, and become yet another enterprise operating in the inherently anarchic surroundings), would it not hold that everyone, including those who work in the unproductive areas of government, would be better off on a relative basis?

The answer, of course, is yes, unless one finds themselves in a position which relies upon the government being able to confiscate a certain amount of resources on their behalf in order to support their livelihood, or finds themselves employed by an enterprise that can only continue to operate with the protection of certain privileges which the mechanism of government may grant them.

However, even this minority would be better off once they adjusted to the reality of life without the idea of government.

What about the Disaster aid, Police and Fire Departments? Aren't they at least indispensible functions of the government?

Of course they are! And for that very reason, private organizations would quickly spring up to replace the government agencies that currently perform these vital roles in society. In fact, they already exist. They are commonly known as Security and Insurance companies. In Anarcho-Capitalist thought, the companies that would arise are called Private Defense Agencies. Anyone skeptical about what would naturally arise in a purely anarchic system to replace functions currently delegated to the State is encouraged to study this theory.

Yet despite the alternatives, the mechanism of the state remains in place and retains a monopolistic power over defense, income redistribution in the form of taxes, as well as the right to generally meddle in all of the affairs of its subjects in the name of promoting security and equality.

As with any failing entity, when a government has gone from being a servant of the people to active enslavement of the populace, its lack of popularity will tend to manifest itself in its own deteriorating financial condition. This fact alone is proof that Anarchy is the context in which the Nation States of the world act and operate. In the final analysis, the world's governments are subject to the same immutable economic laws that individuals and collectives are. On this basis alone it is proper to constantly question the relevancy of the State with regards to its utility against viable alternatives, for both nation states and individuals are equally subject to the forces of natural law.

Next, we will examine the condition of a failing nation-state. It has been observed throughout history that the authorities of a failing nation state or other similar group which has taken for itself a monopoly on defense, rarely give up their arms willingly or peacefully, so it is up to the individual to peacefully disarm it.

For disarming it is the only way that mankind can return to

square one and bravely face the anarchy in which we live. Once we soberly face our anarchic surroundings, it will be clear what is to be done by all, and the tacit communication amongst individuals, commonly referred to as the market, can begin to quickly and efficiently help us to solve our common problems.

How can one go about peacefully disarming an entity that has unilaterally claimed the privilege of maintaining armaments and effective control of other functions which, based on economic imperatives, must necessarily be left to individuals? For practical purposes, we have compiled a brief list of steps that one could take to peacefully resist a non-aggressive nation state that is at peace from within. Each step proposed is a step away from what on the surface appear to be unnecessary rules, and a step towards effectively solving the problems that are a result of our anarchic surroundings:

1. **Money, trade what you want to:** Conduct trade in a currency other than the one used to pay the tax. For it is proper to give to Caesar what is Caesar's, and at the same time, there is no supernatural obligation to use Caesar's money. Render tax declarations only on the amount of trade conducted using the imperial coin and currency.

2. **Rely on common sense**: Ignore laws and other excessive regulations in favor of respect for the free will of those you hire. If someone is willing to work for you for less than minimum wage, allow them to work, do not deprive them of a job to comply with an arbitrary wage rate set by a bureaucrat. Make no conscious distinction between contract workers and employees, for both are performing work, regardless of arbitrary external distinctions implied by laws and regulations.

3. **An important caveat** to this is to not brag about flouting unreasonable laws and regulations. Assume that if

you are breaking a legitimate law, both you and the employee will know of it and have dealt with it long before the government will deal with it. It is the false hope that government is regulating untenable working conditions that gives rise to untenable working conditions in the first place.

4. **Come out of Babylon:** If you live in a place where the microscope of government regulation is unavoidable and unbearable, physically relocate until you have created a safe distance between the regulations and your livelihood.

5. **Cross borders:** If language is not a barrier and your trade or profession is not location specific, there should be no resistance from either government to crossing national borders in search of better opportunities, for all stand to benefit from this.

6. **Sell what consumers want**, not what the government allows you to sell. The greatest test of a product (food included) is public opinion. Government approval of products, like labor laws tend to give the population a false sense of security.

As we have stated above, if the nation state in which one lives operates with intentions that are pure and in harmony with natural law, they should offer no resistance to an individual who chooses to take these steps. Any resistance will come from voluntary actions taken by the individuals who are directly affected, and the natural consequences of failing to do the right thing will fall squarely on one's own shoulders.

If, on the other hand, the nation state begins to pass and enforce laws against these actions, it will have shown itself to be predatory. Far from existing to help people deal with their anarchic surroundings, it will be hindering them from doing so.

Anyone who has attempted to take the steps above has likely encountered some sort of resistance to taking these actions. What may come as a surprise is that the resistance may not have come directly from the government itself, but from disinterested yet well-meaning citizens who have tried to deter these brave souls on the basis of blind obedience to the rules.

What these well-intentioned citizens fail to realize is that blind obedience to the rules makes slaves of everyone.

~~~~~~~~~~~

CONCLUSION

Anarchy is an ultimate given. The rise of the current system of nation states is simply the latest rendition of an attempt by man to bring order to chaos. This latest attempt, like every other attempt at maintaining a far-reaching empire since the dawn of time, is flawed.

For no man or group of men, regardless of their number, clairvoyance, or special powers they profess to have, can suspend or accelerate the operation of natural law. The Creator alone reserves that power for himself.

Viewed from above, nation states are not ultimate givens, and therefore are incapable of spawning natural laws of their own accord. The best they can do is to assist individuals in their common toil to comply with the demands of the state of anarchy in which they live. However, most versions of the nation state, circa 2013, are working on a large-scale basis to at best delay and at worst suppress the ability of the individual to respond to the demands of the natural laws to which we are all subject.

Nation states are merely the prevailing defense agencies in

their geographical region that initially lay claim to the allegiance and a portion of the output of those who are born within their borders. The proof of this fact is in the following: It is true that if one comes to the point of disenchantment with their current nation state, it is possible, yet expensive and perhaps dangerous, to choose amongst which nation state one will submit to. In this sense, nation states can be said to be collective entities that have seized the right to guide a person's response to anarchy at birth. Another proof lies in the manner in which nation states negotiate amongst themselves and with corporations.

Given this understanding of the nation state, it would follow that revolutions are simply extreme reactions to poor customer service, and not a valid claim to a moral high ground as many revolutionaries throughout the ages have professed. When one has a complaint with the way they are being served, the normal response is to take one's business elsewhere, not make an attempt to become CEO of the entity by which they have been treated badly.

We pray that this volume has helped to shatter any preconceived notions regarding Anarchy. For Anarchy is not a boogeyman, rather, it is atheism with regards to government. As such, a state of anarchy does not imply that rules and regulations, which are indispensable for humans to live together in harmony and to plan their daily activities, should be banished.

Anarchy is an ultimate given, and the state of anarchy is constantly in demand of an active response. Due to the urgency felt by all of mankind to respond to the state of anarchy, there will always be rules and regulations. However, a proper understanding of Anarchy as an ultimate given means that persons, instead of being under compulsion to submit to rules and regulations, will voluntarily consent to live by such rules and regulations within a territory or within a certain social sphere because the rules provide an undeniable benefits that all adherents are free to partake in.

While a common response to mankind's inherently anarchic state is always beneficial, an understanding of and appeal to Anarchy, and not allegiance to a corporation or nation state, allows the greater part of mankind to both tacitly and expressly form appropriate responses to anarchy in the present. It will allow lessons learned to disseminate faster and assist more in their chosen response to anarchy than ever before.

For Anarchy is not something to be feared, it is the very essence of freedom.

~~~~~~~~~~~

EPILOGUE: TESTS IN PROGRESS

After reflecting on the ideas that we have presented in this volume, we began to look for evidence of people putting their faith in government to the ultimate test. What we found shocked us. The phenomenon, far from being on the fringe, is already underway in America and throughout much of the world. The following posts, which first appeared on The Mint on August 11, 2011 and July 12, 2012, respectively, explore this interesting phenomenon.

I. IS AMERICA BECOMING UNGOVERNABLE?

{**Editor's note**: This essay first appeared on The Mint on August 17, 2011}

August thoughts in the US are being rudely interrupted by the presidential campaigns that are warming up in Iowa and are heading to New Hampshire to continue the race in which the winner will declare themselves King of the Americans.

As Bloom County fans may recall, when the Meadow party

nominated Bill the Cat and Opus for President and Vice President in 1984, they concluded that only a complete idiot would apply after careful consideration of the job description which, in their estimation, included "*being blamed for every problem on the planet.*"

The complete idiot label came to mind after we heard a comment in a video shared with us by a friend in which Bill Hybels, the Pastor of Willow Creek, a large church in Illinois, noted that the tendency in American dialogue today is to "*throw stones first and ask questions later.*" He explained that people grab onto comments and statements made by others and publicly villianize them without bothering to consider the context or verify the validity of said statements.

His remarks were made at the Willow Global Leadership Summit while addressing the interesting situation in which Howard Schultz, the CEO of Starbucks, backed out of his contract to appear at the summit after receiving threats of a boycott from a group who claimed that Willow Creek was against homosexuals.

Mr. Hybels went on to say that this phenomenon is making America ungovernable.

He did not go into detail as to how the "throw *stones first, ask questions later,*" phenomenon would make the country ungovernable, but the idea got us thinking all the same. What makes a country governable in the first place? Do people naturally need government in order to survive?

In the sense that people need to feel protected and able to care for themselves and their loved ones, people may, at a minimum, need to believe in the concept of government. People, knowing their weak state on this planet, need to believe that someone is looking out for them. This need leads them to subject themselves to the idea of government.

Inevitably, those who are entrusted with embodying the idea of government find that they are given quite a bit of power over the lives of others and quickly learn to abuse it.

This leads the subjects to seek freedom from the government while at the same time looking for someone or something else to fulfill their basic need for physical protection and material well being. Seen this way, when a people become ungovernable, they are rejecting the government that they find themselves subject to because of perceived or actual abuses by or the impotence of the government with regards to fulfilling their needs.

It is important to note that, for people to reach this state, they must feel that they are out of options under their current government. Economic hardship has a lot to do with how people perceive their options, and it should come as no surprise that the level of economic hardship has a positive correlation to the number and reach of laws and policies enacted by governments to restrict the freedoms of individuals.

Free men are infinitely more productive than slaves. And policy changes in either direction will express itself in economic results. Are the people freer or more enslaved as a collective result of the policies in place? The recent economic data coming out of the United States of America prove that we are a people becoming enslaved.

When things go well, no one cares who is governing. When things go badly, they become unnaturally preoccupied with the political process. America, circa 2011, is moving dangerously towards this unnatural preoccupation.

Ironically, the more one concentrates on the government and its political processes, the more it becomes evident that the very existence of a government organized by men may be more of a threat to than a protector of the basic needs of protection and material well-being that have given rise to the concept of government in the first place.

In practice, the governments of the world today operate like competing defense agencies. It may be, then, that Americans are tired of the current contractor and are searching for another one; one that is less intrusive and has fewer overhead costs to cover.

Will they find it before they are completely enslaved by the current one?

II. IS ATHEISM WITH REGARDS TO GOVERNMENT GOING MAINSTREAM?

{**Editor's note**: This essay first appeared on The Mint on July 12, 2012}

We recently subscribed to Gary North's latest project, a site called "The Tea Party Economist." To be clear, we have no political interest nor affiliation, period. It is our feeling that government, in its current state, is best ignored and avoided rather than confronted. If ignored, it will eventually go away, one way or another. While we may have no confidence or belief in government, we make up for it in an abundance of faith in God and our fellow men and women.

To draw on a well known analogy, in our view the Tea Party, together with the Republican and Democratic parties, are fighting for control of the steering wheel of the Titanic after it hit the iceberg. Rather than fight it out on the control deck, we at The Mint realize that the only ones who survived the Titanic were those who found a lifeboat or other means to stay afloat.

Today, Mr. North shared an article on the site which made us gasp. It was written by Jerry Bowyer and, as we read through it, one thought repeatedly passed through our mind: *"Has our manner of thinking really gone mainstream?"*

Mr. Bowyer points out a number of examples of a general decline in voluntary compliance with things that the government increasingly uses its superior force to mandate, such as taxes and environmental laws. The irony is that as a government's power grab via rules and regulations accelerates, voluntary compliance, from which all forms of government ultimately derive their power, declines. It is clear, yet seldom acknowledged, that the absence of voluntary compliance is the most effective type of revolution which can be waged.

If Mr. Bowyer is correct, then it would appear that Americans are taking the idea of atheism with regards to government to heart.

Mr. Bowyer also makes an important distinction which we wish to highlight, for it is very important. The lack of voluntary compliance is not a form of civil disobedience or act of aggression towards a government. Rather, it is the conscious choice to stop believing in the government and live one's life as if it does not exist as anything more than a lethal nuisance to be avoided. Mr. Bowyer eloquently describes this phenomenon via an amoeba metaphor:

"It's not civil disobedience that I'm talking about. It's the opposite: Civil disobedience is meant to be noticed. It is a price paid in the hope of creating social change. What I'm talking about is not based on hope; in fact, it has given up much hope on social change. It thinks

the government is a colossal amoeba twitching mindlessly in response to tiny pinpricks of pain from an endless army of micro-brained interest groups. The point is not to teach the amoeba nor to guide it, but simply to stay away from the lethal stupidity of its pseudopods."

"The amoeba does not get smarter but it does get hungrier and bigger. On the other hand, we get smarter. More and more of our life takes place outside of the amoeba's reach: in the privacy of our own homes, or in capital accounts in other nations, or in the fastest growing amoeba avoidance zone ever created, cyberspace. We revolt decision by decision, transaction by transaction, because we believe deep down that most of what government tells us to do is at bottom illegitimate.[3]"

Everyday, more and more people are recognizing the insanity of attempting to comply with the onslaught of rules and regulations which allegedly protect them against others. They are realizing that the rules are building a prison in which they themselves are incarcerated.

We conclude these thoughts with a quote from Ayn Rand's novel *Atlas Shrugged*, which seems most appropriate when considering an amoeba-like government:

"When you see that trading is done, not by consent, but by compulsion – when you see that in order to produce, you need to obtain permission from men who produce nothing – when you see that money is flowing to those who deal, not in goods, but in favors – when you see that men get richer by graft and by pull than by work, and your laws don't protect you against them, but protect them against you – when you see corruption being rewarded and honesty becoming a self-sacrifice – you may know that your society is doomed."

---

[3] You can read Mr. Bowyer's entire article here at Forbes.com: *July 4th Question, Part III: Americans Revolt Billions of Times a Day* at the following link: http://www.forbes.com/sites/jerrybowyer/2012/07/08/july-4th-question-part-iii-americans-revolt-billions-of-times-a-day/

ATHEISM WITH REGARDS TO GOVERNMENT

~~~~~~~~~~~

ABOUT THE AUTHOR

David is happily married with two children and lives in Portland, Oregon where he has pondered monetary theory and other less pressing but infinitely more entertaining matters since 2006. He has travelled extensively in the United States and has resided in Nebraska, Colorado, Oregon, Spain, and Bolivia.

He has a Bachelors degree in Business Administration from Colorado State University and an MBA from the Universitat de Barcelona, Spain with over 18 years of experience in Accounting, Finance, Treasury, and Information Systems Consulting positions both in the United States and Spain.

He is the creator of The Mint, which presents fresh ideas on Economics, Monetary Theory, and Politics. You can read The Mint at http://www.davidmint.com and you may contact him at davidminteconomics@gmail.com.

www.ingramcontent.com/pod-product-compliance
Lightning Source LLC
Chambersburg PA
CBHW071004290526
45795CB00005B/1775